PEDOPHILES
and YOUR CHILD

By

Peter H. Schmedding

Order this book online at www.trafford.com
or email orders@trafford.com

Most Trafford titles are also available at major online book retailers.

Printed in the United States of America.

ISBN: 978-1-4269-9115-8 (sc)
ISBN: 978-1-4269-9116-5 (hc)
ISBN: 978-1-4269-9118-9 (e)

Library of Congress Control Number: 2011914413

Trafford rev. 08/27/2011

 www.trafford.com

North America & international
toll-free: 1 888 232 4444 (USA & Canada)
phone: 250 383 6864 ♦ fax: 812 355 4082

TABLE OF CONTENTS

Prologue: We have this problem. Now what?................ ix

Introduction: The three aims of this book xi

Chapter One: The making of a pedophile...................... 1

Chapter Two: Under the bonnet of mind 9

Chapter Three: The emergence of the personality 19

Chapter Four: The final answer inside the child 27

If your plan is for a year, plant rice.
If your plan is for a decade, plant trees.
If your plan is for a lifetime, educate children.

- Confucius

PROLOGUE

Peter Schmedding and I have been friends for a number of years. Although my background regarding the subject of Pedophilia is very sparse, I found that what Peter has to say was most interesting. Because of the subject matter, one might be tempted to launch into a diatribe of angry repulsion against pedophiles. Indeed, I found that my first reaction was something between apprehension and disgust. But the problem is real and requires a more careful analysis than simple gut feelings.

The real question is: what can we do to reduce the causes of Pedophilia? Any viable answer must incorporate some type of rational approach along the following lines. We have this problem. As a society, we would probably rather avoid such an unpleasant issue. But to be responsible citizens, it seems that we first have a responsibility to define and face up to the problem. Secondly, we should try to find at least some rational and productive solutions. Perhaps Peter has started a discussion that should be continued.

Robert Stephenson PhD
July 2011

INTRODUCTION

Among the evils in contemporary societies, Pedophilia has taken a prominent place. A wave of suspicion and fear for children's' safety started around the late 1970s in many if not in most countries of the Western world. This was fuelled by revelations of sexual abuse of the young by people who traditionally deserve our unconditional trust.

Statistics on the subject are frightening. For example one study (University of Pennsylvania 2001) found that 47 percent of child molesters were relatives, while 49 percent are neighbours, teachers, coaches and the like. Another study (National Institute of Mental Health 1988) suggests that the typical pedophile molests 117 children on average.

All this, combined with frequent reports of abuse in the media leaves a bitter taste in the minds of many parents.

On the flip side, how much do we have to protect our children from possible molestation without giving them the freedom to take advantage of stimulation by activities beyond home and school?

There is little doubt that chances of success in a future adult life are enhanced by introducing the child to different careers and philosophies by adults from outside the family. Ever so often such people have an influence on the child that exceeds that of even the most caring parent. While in an age of paranoia, not only have extracurricular opportunities become less frequent, whenever they are offered it puts the parent into a double bind. How can they decide if a situation is safe for their child?

The purpose of this book is threefold. The fictional story in the first chapter is derived from a true-to-life experience. It gives one example how inappropriate attitudes and outmoded practices can actually create pedophiles.

Secondly it takes a closer look inside the mind of such offenders. As any attempt to explain the working of the human brain by outlining neuronal processes would lead us into a jungle, instead, with the use of analogies and more case histories, from different perspectives it shows how our personalities are shaped for success or failure by our surroundings from the earliest days.

Thirdly, what about our children? How do we decide if we should permit them to take part in a certain activity or establishing a relationship outside the family?

It may be impossible to give an answer that covers all possibilities. A number of guide lines, however, will direct us toward a more considerate and relatively safe decision. The final answer after all may well be within the child him or herself.

Finally, it is unfortunate that the word Pedophile has established itself as the sexual exploitation of children, m fact even in languages other than English. Do we talk about the hetereophile, the biphile or the homophile? As we normally take 'heterosexual' etc. as accepted expressions, similarly an appropriate word would have been: 'Pedosexual'. I consider words such as pedophile and pedophilia as misleading and damaging.

A pedophile (child lover) in the proper sense would never harm children in any way. They would do their best to support them on the way toward a successful adulthood. I am using that word under protest and only to not add more confusion to this very unfortunate chapter in human behaviour.

In summary, whenever this phenomenon raises its head the common reactions are feelings of anger and revenge. Because they do not help us in any way, in this book we put those emotions aside. It has been written in simple language for anyone who wishes to explore the subject more deeply, its causes, prevention and possible solutions.

Peter H Schmedding
Canberra Australia
July 2011

A necessary preface to chapter one.

Is this the hardest pill to swallow? Could it be true that in certain cases – albeit without intending or even being aware of it – pedophiles are created? Then, years later, when their crimes have come to light and their victims have been damaged we put the perpetrators into jail?

One variation on that very theme is described in this chapter.

This preface to chapter one has been an afterthought. Its inclusion seemed necessary in order to guard against readers and critics who will accuse the author of making excuses or even condoning molestation and rape of children. This book is not about accusing or excusing. This book's aim is to seek prevention, protection and solutions.

CHAPTER ONE

"I have never had a friend in all my life".

That was Eric's first comment. At the time I was a part-time volunteer counsellor, mostly in sexuality matters for young people. In that position, Eric, moving toward middle age, was not really the sort of person I was used to dealing with.

Even after all the years that have passed in between I still remember my impression of Eric as he came to his first consultation. His neat dress did not harmonise with his facial expression. He looked grim. I could not help wondering if he had ever smiled in his life.

From experience we know that the real reason for a client to ask for help is seldom revealed. Deeply seated complexes or feelings of guilt, secret phobias or deviations from what is considered the norm are seen as too risky to be disclosed, at least at the beginning of such encounters. Rather it is common for most clients to find a more acceptable symptom that is presented as the reason to seek help and advice.

I tried to hide my impatience as we talked for some time and seemed to go around in a circle, repeating and repeating the old story: No friend – ever. It was obvious, there was an secret issue that Eric was not willing to talk about.

Although to my mind we had made no progress whatsoever in this first session he seemed to be very keen to come again. He insisted that we made another appointment right there and then.

This time he talked more freely about some of his wrong doings, his failures in life. He seemed amazed that I did not react in a disapproving manner. Moving toward me he suddenly whispered: "You know, I have been in jail..." As soon as the words came out his hand covered his mouth, leaning back defensively. Did he expect me to hit him?

"You have been in jail." My emotionless tone of voice, free from any accusation or surprise seem to have lifted a load from his shoulders. Now he was able to talk more easily, however, he changed the subject to unrelated matters. He seemed to be in a hurry to get away and again insisted on making the next appointment. Before leaving, however, he said:

"You know, I had sex with young boys".
"Then they found out about it and put you in jail?"
"Yes. Then they put me in jail." With a sigh of relief he left.

I thought back to my own childhood. As a four or six year old, on a couple of occasions I was warned not to take any lollies from a certain man somewhere around our neighbourhood. "Never talk to him and if he approaches you, run away". As there was no further explanation I was confused. I had never met this certain man but I remembered the anxiety I had felt should some stranger ever have approached me, talked to me or offered me some sweets.

Now I had met Eric. Was he the 'stranger', reincarnated?

During those years I was a member of the then Society of Sex Educators, Researchers and Therapists. In all our activities we had never discussed sexual activities between adults and children, so I was interested if a man (or a woman, for that matter) who had the urge to sexually interact with the young is an inherited trend or is it something that is allowed to develop in the mind, possibly from early childhood. Would Eric be able to provide some answers?

After the third session Eric and I had developed a trusting relationship. I suspected I might have been the only person who ever in his life was willing to listen to him and take him seriously. I arranged a few meetings outside the consultation room. We met a few times for an afternoon cup of coffee or simply for a walk in the open air. Bit by bit the story of his early life unfolded.

Eric's mother was unmarried or divorced. She hated men. She hated men with a passion. She wanted a child. Of course it had to be a girl. Her prayers were not answered. When the baby arrived it was a he. Not surprisingly Eric had no conscious recollection of his earliest days. As he became aware of his surroundings, his main memory was a steady feeling of resentment, of hostility.

As the meaning of words and speech developed, he remembered mother's expressions of how useless boys are. "Boys are dirty." "Boys are mean." "Boys are bad". Those and similar expressions had now become Eric's daily mental diet.

In his childish way he had made attempts to be good. As he grew older, even trying to behave like a girl did not have any effect on his mother's attitude toward him. Realising that nothing he could do to gain mother's affection or at least approval, he gave up. Why did she give life to a child as she hated him so much? There was no-one to ask, no-one to give an answer. He felt betrayed, helpless.

His lack of self confidence made him behave in ways that his school mates ostracised him. He was not allowed to invite any of his peers to his home. He was never able to establish a friendship. There were no birthday parties or invitations for Eric.

By the time he was around ten years old, his mind was made up: Females are enemies. The feeling of hostility he was exposed to from his early days now was directed toward females. He had grown to hating 'all the opposite sex'. For fear of hitting out one day he avoided coming too close to them.

The lack of a male model during his developing years was a significant factor that led to his feeling of worthlessness and emotional isolation. Then he discovered that he could accept and be accepted by boys much younger than he was at the time. He enjoyed meeting them and talking with them. That intensified over the years and finally lead to his demise.

My last memory of Eric was watching him selling ice cream in a kiosk. He made no attempt to hide his expression of bitterness. If his face could have talked it would have accused every one of his mostly women customers for just being there.

I rang up to arrange another meeting. A woman answered the phone: "They carried him away this morning. He died of a heart attack." So ended my association with the man who never in his life had a friend.

Looking back, Eric had approached me in the hope of finding that one person who could give him the comfort of reaching out to another human being, of understanding him in his isolation. I believe I was able to give him that comfort. To me, however, Eric had become an important teacher. He had added yet another piece in the jigsaw puzzle that has been in my mind for most of my life: The emergence of the personality. He became an example of how a life can be wasted. A tragic loss I will remember for the rest of my days.

I gave a speech to an audience one day. I spoke about the life and death of Eric. Last sentence:

"... and so I accepted Eric, the pedophile, posthumously as my friend."

Chapter Two

*B*efore continuing please note: This treatise on the topic of the pedophile may be considered wordy and going into too many side issues. I make no apologies for this. If you find it long-winded, this text may not be for you. The pedophile is one manifestation of tragic flaws in today's society. Only a more comprehensive investigation and looking at the issue from different angles can help us to understand the problem, how it is caused and how we can defend ourselves and our children against harassment, abuse and exploitation

Imagine a nicely built brick wall. It may be six or eight feet high. Or two metres, if you like. All the bricks fit together neatly and the mortar joints are even, all 10 mm thick. As the bricks are all the same shape and size, the wall looks just perfect. It is 'well formed', to borrow an expression from the Neuro Linguistic Programmers.

But now imagine that a similar brick wall had, maybe as far down as in the first or second layer one brick that has been put down at a queer angle or was shaped like a rock. As a result the wall right to the top would be 'ill formed'. No matter how we would try to remedy the out-of-shape portions of the wall, it would never look as nice as the one I mentioned first. In a proper building it would have to be pulled down and rebuilt.

In the first chapter I gave the account of Eric, a true to life experience. Here we had a man whose mind was perverted, it became 'ill formed' from his earliest days. This continued throughout his school years. His feelings of inferiority prevented him from establishing any sort of friendship. He was ridiculed and ostracised by his peers. A wasted life to the end.

What is the correlation between brick walls and pedophiles? What is the difference?

What went wrong with the faulty brick wall is clear. We can SEE it, we can examine it. By contrast, if similar faults have created emotional abnormalities in early childhood, in the adult we CAN NOT SEE IT. The causes of a corrupted mind are long forgotten. With the causes out of sight we only blame the now adult.

THAT is the missing link in personality development.

As a rule we will never be able to completely divorce ourselves from conditionings we were subjected to in our childhood years. The list of personality disorders seems endless. It includes cruelty, wife and child bashing, sexual perversions. They lead to inhuman acts by leaders such as Hitler or Stalin or Pol Pot.

Oh yes, the list includes pedophiles.

One sentence I read somewhere comes to mind (from memory): 'How much better would the world have been if those ruthless leaders of countries and criminals had a good male model when they were children.' The experience of Eric supports a notion that the same applies to all boys.

Summarising all the above in different words: The personality from its earliest years (from conception, but that's another story) is built up from experiences. If those experiences fit together in a 'well formed' manner, the person will grow feeling good about him/herself and so has the best chance to become a useful citizen. If the experiences are adverse, the person is more likely to join the league of misfits and criminals that compromise a civilised society.

And that brings me to my point:

1) Do we always realise how much the personality of the future adult depends on what they have experienced going back to their earliest days?

2) Does the case of Eric, cited earlier, demonstrate how we would go about if we wished to rear a child to become a sexual deviant, a child molester or an otherwise socially defective adult?

3) Out of countless, related examples take this one: Could it be true that many sexual cripples who are able to have a fulfilling experience with a prostitute, but are unable to relate in this way to their own wives, have been conditioned in similar ways? If sex has been imprinted in their minds as 'dirty' then an attitude like 'MY WIFE is clean and would never... I have to go to a house of low repute to really have the great experience...' may well be the outcome.

(Yes, I have come across such cases.)

It is by no means a conscious decision. It is an irresistible behaviour pattern originating from damaging programming early in life. Once imprinted it will grow in the mind like a weed and in time overshadow all the logic and remedies that may be tried to effect a cure. In the words of one authority (Dr. Lee Salk, 1972): "...emotional problems created very early in life and abnormal patterns of behaviour established at that time ... even major psychotherapy is frequently unsuccessful."

Before continuing I wish to make this statement. By outlining these hypotheses I am not condoning or excusing any acts of child molestation whatsoever. Individuals unable to overcome the urge of relieving their sexual needs in the body of a child I would like to see separated from society. My contention in this series is to put a different view on the subject of the pedophile. How we deal with the problem and, in the long run, what can we do to help avoiding it? What about our children? How can these issues be carried over into many other areas of human experience?

One sentence that impressed me all my life has been attributed to Shakespeare: "All the world is a stage..." Could it be true that in the final analysis we are all actors on an imagined stage? That we are given the role of a certain character and forced to play it on that stage and throughout our lives? Could it be that our belief that this role **is reality** (instead of the result of misguided programming) is misleading us without us being aware of it?

If the answers to these questions were no, how could it be possible to create people such as the religious fanatic, the serial killer or the committed pedophile? If the answers are yes, then we might as well ask: What are the factors that lead to such misguided attitudes and behaviours in the first place?

We can learn about it by looking into the vast material of case histories that exists to show how the minds of our young can be perverted, even with the best intentions. It is, however, more rewarding if we also examine the methods that enrich our and our children's lives.

Case one. This is a hypothetical case.

One young boy asked his dad what the word 'penis' meant. With a matter-of-fact attitude Dad explained that the penis is a part of the human body. Only boys and, of course, men have a penis. As this is a very private part of us we do not talk about that outside the family. But you know that you always ask me about such things and I will always be happy to give you the right answer. Is there anything else you wish to know?

As a rule, young children don't. They are not interested in details. The child's curiosity has been satisfied and the case, for the time being, is closed. But there is more. The process has positive side effects. The child now knows that, no matter how embarrassing a topic may seem to be, he has developed the trust that he can always go and ask his dad. Beyond that there is an element of safety. That means if another, less enlightened child might tell him some distorted, misguided facts of life, he may well shrug it off. He knows better. He is protected from unsuitable material.

"Ignorance is never bliss", said noted sexologist Sol Gordon.

Case two. This came from a collection of case histories, part of my study material years ago.

One young boy asked his dad what the word 'penis' meant. As the report stated, in response he was brutally beaten by his Dad for "using such a word".

Only one such incident will destroy the sense of trust in the child. This child is not likely to ever dare to ask his father again in matters of sex and procreation. To him, questioning in this way means severe punishment. No explanation. Only confusion and fear. His mind has been perverted.

This case is a nasty one, although nothing out of the ordinary if we look into the cruelties that children had to endure over the centuries. Now to my next point.

A complex such as this, even though it may be less dramatic than the last case, tends to expand in the mind of the child. It now extends to lack of trust to adults generally. It distorts the structure of feelings and knowledge in the mind as the child grows older. It leads to guilt and confusion when feelings of a sexual nature emerge. Above I mentioned the case of the husband, unable to relate to his wife. This is one outcome of damaging programming in the early years. A different outcome may well be the complex to relate sexually only to children. Sexual feelings are as natural and necessary as hunger and thirst. In addition, repress those feelings with all sorts of fear-inducing myths and you have the perfect recipe to produce the pedophile.

Are there any solutions?

Before embarking on the next chapter let me repeat these two points: 1) Do we first create the pedophile, then, after they possibly ruined the lives of their victims, prosecute them? Secondly, while outlining these theories, in no way do I excuse or condone, ever, sexual exploitation of children.

CHAPTER THREE

*O*ne of the most memorable impressions of my childhood was a wall hanging in my bedroom. Even before I could read I admired the beautifully hand-stitched letters in red and yellow on a white background. As I began to learn the meaning of letters and words from age five or so, over the months (years?) bit by bit I deciphered the meaning of that message and interpreted what they meant to me.

I had lost my parents at an early stage and there was no one in my life I was able to talk to about my concerns. That must have been the reason why I absorbed those words with eagerness. Those letters seem to talk to me.

The language was rather poetic. An attempt to translate it into English most likely would distort the meaning and yet it sounded simple: "...Es ist so schoen zu sorgen..." (It is so nice to care)... to care, for others, for someone. It suggested to me a feeling of peace and gratitude should I ever be able to create something, to help someone... somewhere... somehow... I could hardly imagine what it could have been. It became a hazy concept and yet had etched itself deeply into my memory banks.

Much later, in adulthood it had solidified. More like a firm belief it became my 'role' on the 'stage of life', quoting Shakespeare once more. An irresistible blueprint it had become a part of my personality.

Considering the lack of sensible guidance I had experienced as a child, those poetic words gave me meaning and direction. What would have become of me if the wall hanging instead had said: "Life is for enjoyment... You have a right to take whatever you desire... Live and take what you are entitled to or you will lose out..."?

What would I have become if there was a message of perversities or hellfire, brimstone and fear-inducing creatures?

What would I have become if someone from my earliest days had shown hostility, rejection and the constant barrage of (remember from the first chapter, the story of Eric?) comments such as 'Boys are dirty... useless... mean...'?

Let us look at this concept from a different perspective.

We all agree that, to explain mind functions in a technical// biological way – how the neurones communicate with others by tiny electric and chemical signals – would be tedious, meaningless and take lots of time. Even moving a little finger or calculating a sum involves thousands of neurones communicating with others in different parts of the brain. Models in the form of metaphors overcome this problem and give us some understanding. Let me explain.

A computer needs an operating system (OS) to function. This OS has been programmed by specialists in the field. Can a similarity been drawn between the computer's OS and the human mind? The examples above show how the OS inside our brains can be programmed, like the OS of a computer, to either operate successfully or has limitations if not even dysfunctions that lead to disaster. Let us have a closer look at this OS.

We know that we possess a conscious mind and an unconscious mind. How do they interact?

Imagine an ocean liner. To pay a visit into the engine department is an unforgettable experience. The size of the engines, the noise, the power are overwhelming. Thousands of horse power drive the ship across the ocean.

Above, up on the bridge the captain signals to the engine room. He dictates the direction and the speed the vessel is to travel. Without the co-operation of the engine department, no matter how fast the captain would perhaps try to paddle, it would make no impression on the movement of the ship.

To follow this model further, please also note: The people who operate the engines in the bowels of the ship are – regarding where the ship goes – blind. Furthermore, if during the construction of the ship perhaps a faulty part of the steering mechanism has mistakenly been placed and consequently the steering gets stuck one day, the ship may be forced to travel in a never ending circle. Is it now right and proper to blame the captain?

If we can accept this simplified model as an explanation how the human mind functions we might get a glimpse into the mysterious ways what makes us tick.

The conscious mind is the captain of our life. The unconscious is the vastly more powerful power house of our personality. Like a library it has a reservoir of experiences, hurts, pleasures, hopes, facts, opinions, expectations, beliefs bordering on the infinite. It remembers the comments and conditionings we have been exposed to. The summary of all those factors become us, they are our personality.

If the conscious mind communicates efficiently with the 'well formed' (this expression again) unconscious mind, we have the best chance leading a successful life. If this unconscious mind has been perverted or has been misguided and/or damaged during its construction, we can expect the later emerging personality be dysfunctional. To morals, justice and achievements the unconscious is largely blind. It is the computer inside us. It operates in the way it has been programmed. Comes to mind the common expression: Garbage in - garbage out.

Likewise, we are all aware of the damage a virus can do – in a computer, and so in the mind. Sometimes the damage may just be a nuisance. At other times the damage can be severe. It may even grow as time goes on.

What are those viruses some children are exposed to?

Generally all put-downs, insults, discouragement's and belittling comments. More specifically, where sex and procreation is concerned, leading to sexual dysfunction in adulthood and so in certain cases to the creation of future pedophiles: Anxiety, secrecy, fear, shame, isolation (no-one to talk to and get advice) ridiculing children's genitals, blaming for imagined or real wrong-doings... belong to those factors that poison the mind. They develop into powerful emotions over which the individual finally has no control.

"The answer is prevention, eliminating the causes of emotional disturbances and preventing the occurrence of debilitating illnesses...", quoting once more Dr. Lee Salk (1973) "... What shocks me is that so little emphasis has been placed on services to prevent and diagnose emotional health problems... relatively little effort is directed toward assisting those who are primarily responsible for the personality development of infants and young children – their parents."

In spite of our liberal attitudes these days the taboo about sex is still deeply ingrained in many people's minds. The fact is, children will want to know. They seek answers and will find answers. The problem is: From whom? I heard this sentence somewhere: 'How sad that children have to find porn to satisfy their curiosity how the human body works.' Another comment I came across more recently: "I learnt things from other kids, often in a distorted way as the subject was too taboo for my parents."

Prevention of mind perversions in these matters demands **honesty by parents.**

The younger the child, the easier is for them it to accommodate the differences between human bodies. But also, the easier is it to create shame, guilt and confusion in the child. If, say, while coming out of the shower we anxiously cover ourselves up to prevent the child seeing us naked, we already giving this clear message: Here is something shameful that must not be seen or talked about. While there is no need to parade one's private parts through the family home, hiding deliberately leads to suspicion of something being wrong. If the five year old asks a question and we show anxiety and embarrassment, we have given a negative message even before uttering a single word.

Treating the subject with simplicity is the answer. There is no such thing as a stupid question. Unfortunately, there are stupid answers. If the seven year old asks what the word 'penis' means... Well I have covered that already in the previous chapter.

Such a positive change in attitude in time will prevent many from developing into pedophiles. But there is still one fly in the ointment: There **are** such people in the world. How do we defend ourselves and our children?

That will be one of the issues in the following chapter.

CHAPTER FOUR

---

*T*hose who ever had an interest in the "nurture or nature' debate will know that certain life programs are inherited. Examples are the psychopath, the musical genius, the compulsive gambler, the inventor, the survivor, the pessimist and so the list continues.

How does this relate to the pedophile issue?

It seems certain that there are people who have been predisposed genetically to become sexually attracted to children in preference to adults. They are 'born' that way and any intervention or treatment is unlikely to affect a cure. And as long as their aim is to find relief from sexual tensions in the body of a child, frankly, I do not care how they got into that mindset. Anyone who rapes or otherwise exploits children sexually I would like to see put into some sort of cage where it would not be possible for them to ever come near a child again. It is similar to murderers. We put them away without regard as to how they got into such a position.

There is, however, a sinister flip side to the coin:

We will never know how many of our world's children have been actually **raised** to become pedophiles. To my knowledge this is a topic that has not found its way into the media nor does it appear of interest to anyone working in the field. To illustrate, recently I heard about the following case: An adult male had confessed: "I could never have sexual intercourse with a woman, even if they paid me a high sum of money." After a string of sessions with a psychotherapist he finally was able to recall the long forgotten first sex education he had received as a young child. Another just a little older child explained to him the difference between boys and girls. He described the female genitalia as a foul stinking piece of meat, adding the worst adjectives he could think of. Now in his early thirties the 'ex pupil' shuddered at the thought of ever having sex with a woman.

This example shows how early impressions - consciously - are forgotten or repressed while their emotional sting may follow them into the ripe adult years. A compulsion forces the individual to obey a stimulus that took place at a time long forgotten. It has become a part of the person's personality.

How many children at an impressionable age have been conditioned in ways similar to the one mentioned in the above paragraph? Even in our time, how often is everything 'down there' described as dirty and shameful? Or fear is instilled by explaining that sex is a sin and will be punished accordingly? How many kids would dare to mention to either of their parents that they have sexual feelings and how to deal with them? How many children hide their feelings - and activities - from parents, indeed from adults in general? After all, they have found there is nobody willing to listen and take their concerns seriously.

While some of those are less affected, how many become sexual cripples? And out of those, for how many does a broad path lead to **becoming** pedophiles?

In many Western nations a witch hunt has developed during the last decades, a paranoia where anybody showing an interest in working with children is suspected of having sinister motives. This is reflected in absurd measures that have been created to protect children from the evils of sexual predators. The children, in turn, become aware of this. Having been exposed to the paranoia, many may well grow up into a suspicious, hostile next generation. Furthermore, their progress in the preparation for life that could be achieved by youth leaders, volunteers and mentors is lost.

If my hunch is correct it appears that, at least in the long run, one measure to stem pedophilia is to take a new approach in the education of our children. When discarding outmoded beliefs and maintaining honesty in the facts of life from an early age becomes the norm we will have come a long way toward a future, sexually mature society where children grow up feeling safe. That, however, will find much opposition and controversy and take many years. As we are not willing to wait that long, how can we protect our children from harm – now?

Let us summarise the important conclusions from all the discussions so far:

1. How do we identify a pedophile? The trap is that they often parade their charm and genuine concern for kids to everyone who is willing to listen. Free from any guilt, they will offer help and gifts and all the care for a child, while evil intentions are lurking behind the facade of trust and concern.

To be aware of those characteristics takes us some of the way toward considering safety with our children.

2. Is it possible to identify with reasonable certainty those people who are genuine and have the natural motivation to teach children and support them on the way to adulthood?

Most, if not all people who may interact with your child have a reputation. Offenders as a rule have offended more than only once. By contrast, their positive involvement with children in the past will guide us. In fact, the safest indicator may well be the person's past history in working with children. Beyond that, for the parent it is desirable to establish honest and trusting communication with any mentor or volunteer. Their task is to be a support to the parent rather than take away any of the parent's rights in the care of the child.

3. How can we be absolutely sure if our child is safe with a particular person?

I don't know if there is a definite answer. What I do suggest is that there are ways to be certain to the extent that missed opportunities for the child's advancement would do more harm than the (theoretically possible, but extremely unlikely) event of him or her being molested. This, combined with the natural defence instilled by honesty in matters of sex and procreation, and knowing how to protect oneself, should make any danger of abuse virtually non-existent.

That leads to my last point: **The solution is in the child him/herself.**

1. The protected child needs to know that....

... certain adults can be sick, not only physically but also in their mind. Some pretend to be good people but are not.

... we do not poke our fingers into a child's eyes or ears or mouth. Similarly we do not allow parts inside our pants to be touched or manipulated. It is any child's right to say: "No!" And a child's wish to discontinue the relationship will be respected.

... they realise the danger when they are being threatened by: "Don't tell your mum" or "... if you tell anyone..." (the more dreadful, the greater the danger!) They know that the safe way is to go to the parent or carer or other adult person with whom they have established a level of trust and tell.

Finally...

... they know how to avoid unsafe situations. They will feel safe when interacting alone with, say, a new teacher or mentor they had not met before, it takes place with an escape route such as an open door. One example would be when a stranger invites the child to get into the car because "your mother asked me to take you home."

The protected child has been taught how to act without becoming paranoid and distrustful of people in general, thus allowing him or her to be involved in relationships and activities that enriches their lives beyond the school experience.

A closing word.

The reader may have noticed that in this, as well as in the forgoing chapters, from different perspectives I have repeated and illustrated one process: the key for a better and more productive life of the future adult – and in a wider sense for a more harmonious and progressive next generation – lies in the programming of our children from their earliest days. It starts at conception, although this is a different study and not under discussion here.

This repetition has been deliberate. I consider that topic as one of the underrated, unrecognised social issues generally. It extends far beyond the primary purpose of this publication. In that sense, I also believe, when the problem of pedophilia has been put into a proper balance, other destructive issues such as emotional abuse and put-downs, mental cruelty and physical neglect that affects children for the rest of their lives will be given the attention they deserve.

* * *